C000149023

from EMBRACING THE SPARROW-WALL or 1 SCHUMANN-MADNESS

OOMPH! Press © 2019

This English language translation is published under First Serial Rights. Original author, publisher, & translator retain full copyright.

The original German language text, *vom Umhalsen der Sperlingswand, oder 1 Schumannwahnsinn*, by Friederike Mayröcker, ©Suhrkamp Verlag Berlin 2011, was provided under a non-exclusive reprint permission.

This book is set in Garamond, Cocogoose, & Bell Gothic STD. Cover image provided by the author.

Book Layout & Cover Design by Laura Theobald
Edited by Daniel Beauregard & Alex Gregor

For a complete listing of titles please visit www.oomphpress.com.

from **EMBRACING THE SPARROW-WALL** or **1 SCHUMANN-MADNESS**

FRIEDERIKE MAYRÖCKER

TRANSLATED BY JONATHAN LARSON

ACKNOWLEDGMENTS

Grateful acknowledgment is given to Dylan Byron, editor at *Associating Poetry*, where excerpts from this translation appeared.

A NOTE FROM THE TRANSLATOR

For the last three-quarters of a century, Friederike Mayröcker has established her name as a world-force of literature, having published upwards of 100 titles that include radio plays, librettos, children's books, and works of ungenred poetry and prose. She spent most of her working career as an English teacher in Vienna before she was able to take an early retirement in 1969, after which she committed herself to a life of full-time writing. Around that same time the poet Ernst Jandl—Mayröcker's "heart-and-hand companion" until his death in 2000—was approached about producing audio plays for the radio, four of which he would collaborate with Mayröcker on while they continued their various book projects. Since then she has written just over thirty radio plays of her own, this collection initially being one of them before it was published in book form as the textual record.

The form of the German language radio play—*Hörspiel*, which translates literally to "audio play" or "listening play" in English, would be mostly unfamiliar to English language listeners as something heard on the radio since it has a lot more in common with sound art and sound poetry than radio dramas. It is characteristic for these plays to collage voice overs, polyvocalisms, soundscapes, stereophony, musical interludes and accompaniments, analogue and digital sound effects, i.e. a musique concrète that also includes the voiced text as a compositional element. Not only did these radio plays provide a surplus stream of income for writers, but they also allowed and encouraged writing that dialed up the acoustics and punning—the melopoeiac frequencies of charged sound—as a way of counteracting western linear syntactic conventions that spoke in terms of subject-verb object. In her acceptance speech for the oldest radio play award, the radio play prize of the

war blinded, which she received together with Jandl for *Fünf Mann Menschen* (*Five Man Humans*), Mayröcker described the radio play as "calling up a distinct reaction from the listener, something that shares an affinity with musical pleasure, but is sparked by words and noises instead of notes [Tönen]." Even though Mayröcker has said that audio plays serve only as a side lane to her writing, the generative influence the form has had on her prose work, in particular, is evident in the crowding of voices, eavesdropped snatches of dialogue and recollection, ambient sounds, and above all, musicality coming together as a textual fugue from that point on. We witness the lyrical I qua microphone.

In that vein, the first rendition of what eventually became this chapbook was initially titled *from Embracing the Composer on the Open Sofa*, which Mayröcker performed on stage with her friend and fellow artist Bodo Hell, who intoned echoes and susurrous undertunes to Mayröcker's reading for their live public sound performances during the summer of 2010 in Vienna. The project was then made into the radio play *1 Schumann-madness*, which received its third life by Mayröcker's publisher, Suhrkamp Verlag, when it appeared on the page with the title of this book. The 19th Century composer and graphomaniac Robert Schumann and the pianist and composer Clara Schumann feature alongside Jandl and the poet herself as central figures in this recital, or perhaps even serve as each other's doppelgängers, with anecdotal evidence and lines from their lives and letters interwoven. Robert Schumann's diary entries set up the source motif, their relations of sexual experience, personal medical history, and artistic musing are all flush sampling materials for Mayröcker to recompose a new text from an old one, as if it were written as a reinterpretation of Robert Schumann's diaries ("1 has to feel it, 1 has to feel language, to lay on or take off 1 weight here and there like pharmacist scale, so it must sound, so *tuned* ").

The piece was itself initially conceived as musical performance. Cutting up musicians' biographies first became a mode of textual production in Mayröcker's groundbreaking 1978 prose collection *Heiligenanstalt* (translated into English for *Burning Deck* by Rosmarie Waldrop) in which the musings of Chopin, Brahms, Robert and Clara Schumann, Bruckner and Schubert are interwoven with first person accounts. Mayröcker's 2009 collection *Scardanelli* (which I translated into English for The Song Cave) similarly re-tapestries lines from Hölderlin's biography, letters, and poems to induce a Rimbaldian "I is another" orientation, a technique prevalent throughout Mayröcker's oeuvre, whether in drawing on telephone conversations with artist friends, the piano playing of Glenn Gould, invoking the works of Francis Bacon, Francesca Woodman, or Cy Twombly, or writing in response to Jacques Derrida, Gertrude Stein, or Francis Ponge. Because this text overruns with resonance and reference, deriving from a (re)visionary incantation of Robert Schumann's lifestyle, I've endeavored to convey each phrasing with a corresponding density and grain of phrasing so that it might carry Mayröcker's tune, even if that means I'm missing some notes, but, thankfully for the reader, the original score is also reproduced here to play Mayröcker's "cloud of sound" in stereo.

This translation is lovingly dedicated to my mother, DeeDee Feller Larson.

— J.L.
February, 2019
Brooklyn

VOM UMHALSEN DER SPERLINGSWAND MITTEN IM EPHEU

ob die nasse Wäsche in der Kammer und an Silvie denkend was
sie mir gutes an jenem Tag als ER begraben wurde getan dasz sie
bei mir schlief in jener Nacht weil ich Angst hatte allein zu
bleiben und die Komposition »an Silvia« von Franz Schubert
die mir geisterte weil ich hatte viel geweint und der Winter
tappte gegen die Scheiben nämlich die tappende Jahreszeit und
er beugte sich zu mir und flöszte mir Trost ich meine so klammern
wir uns an Strohhalm so weinen wir in der Kammer so sehen wir
zu wie alles zu Unrat wird und die Strähnen der Haare weiszt du
sie kleben von Honig dasz der Morgen. So geweint so weinend so
starrend von Unrat so mit *ausgebüschelten* Flügeln und Armen die
gebratene Menschenhaut dasz sie verzehrte die Speise auf ihrem
Teller und die verwirrten Hunde schnappten, die sanften Doggen
aus ihrer Kindheit während Erschütterungen von Licht und die Pfade
von einer Bude zur anderen dasz mir die Tränen = die Honigtropfen
dasz mir die Trübnisse : Dunkelrosen der Nacht

10. 1. 2010

FROM EMBRACING THE SPARROW-WALL AMID THE IVY

whether the wet laundry in my chamber and thinking of Silvie what
all she requited to me on that day when HE was buried she slept
beside me that night because I was afraid to remain
alone and the composition »to Silvia« by Franz Schubert
which haunted me because I had cried a lot and the winter
tapped against the glass namely the tapping time of year and
he bent down to me and laved consolation I mean so we cling
to straw so we cry in our chamber so we look on as
all turns to filth and the strands of hair you know
they're sticky with honey that the morning. So cried so crying so
stiffened with filth so with *tufted-out* wings and arms the
fried human skin that she devoured the meal on her
plate and the confused dogs snapped up, the gentle mastiffs
from her childhood while tremors of light and the paths from
one dive to another that tears to me = the honey drops that
sorrows to me : dark roses of the night

10. 1. 2010

Wenn 1 Person fehlt (ausgespart ist) auf einer Fotografie, dann sind nur die Umrisse dieser Person zu sehen also ihre Aussparung, sei es dasz es sich um eine gestorbene Person handelt sei es dasz es 1 afrikanische Person ist die fotografiert worden war ohne ohne deren Zustimmung, dasz die Person vorausgesagt hat dasz sie auf der Fotografie nicht sichtbar sein würde etc. Diese *Aussparungen* von Personen finden sich gerne auf Fotografien von Familiengruppen, viele Kerbtiere, Schatten, Seelen, transparente Hüllen DER AUGENSCHEIN UNS BESCHIRMET dank der *wundertätigen* Pianistin (Clara) ist unendlich viel in Bewegung geraten zwischen Berlin Wien Innsbruck und Meran. Ich schwebe tagelang in Musik, so Ezra Pound, mir geht es jetzt so sonderbar gut, hingerissen von den Klaviermusiken des Komponisten aus 3 Himmelsrichtungen, mit meinen Händen, Schritten *(mit aufgepflanzten Gladiolen)*, Kugelfischen, Laternen, Santa Lucia = diese Passage von Siegfried Höllrigl usw.

Ich war erloschen, in gefälligem Wahnsinn versunken, sie hatte sich nur 1 wenig erbrochen, der Komponist sagte zu mir, wie entschuldigend, *die Clara sei 1 biszchen schwanger* – als wir im Foyer des Gartenbaukinos ehe die Vorstellung began die Flamm' sagt der Komponist, und seh die Sonn' vorüberflieg'n, der Komponist sagt mir er habe mit Blixa Baargeld ein Interview gemacht, so wie Hungernde Baumrinde essen, so die Vereinsamten = die einsame Seele : Bücher, Sätze und Worte, Musiken, die Abendröte, den Fliederbaum. Die speichelnasse Manschette um den Schneeglöckchenstrausz ist getrocknet, sagt die Pianistin, des Komponisten Hemdmanschette – wir sind schweigend einander gegenübergesessen, sagt mir die Pianistin, haben neuen Versen von Ferdinand Schmatz gelauscht, während der Komponist mir ein belegtes Brot (mit Unrat belegtes Brot) über den Tisch reicht welches ich zusammenklappe. Der Komponist verläszt den Raum und steigt auf das Fenster im Korridor um sich in die Tiefe zu stürzen, ich fasse ihn an den Beinen, ziehe ihn zurück – die Pianistin sagt, *habe heu-*

When 1 person is missing (left blank) on a photograph, then the mere outlines of this person can be seen i.e. their blank space, whether it pertains to a deceased person whether it pertains to 1 African person who has been photographed without their consent, whether the person had predicted that they wouldn't be visible on the photograph etc. These *blank spaces* of persons are happily found on photographs of family groups, many insects, shadows, souls, transparent shells THE EYE'S APPEARING SHIELDS US thanks to the *wonder-working* pianist (Clara) an infinite lot was set in motion between Berlin Vienna Innsbruck and Meran. I float for days on end in music, so says Ezra Pound, now I'm doing exceedingly well, enthralled by the composer's piano-musics from 3 cardinal directions, with my hands, steps *(with planted-on gladiolas)*, blowfish, lanterns, Santa Lucia = this passage of Siegfried Höllrigl etc.

I was extinct, submerged in pleasant madness, she'd thrown up only a little, the composer said to me, as if apologetic, that Clara was a bit pregnant—while we in the foyer of the Gartenbaukino until the presentation began the flame says the composer, and see the sun flying past, the composer tells me he'd interviewed Blixa Baargeld, just as the starving eat treebark, so the lonesome = the lonely soul : books, sentences and words, musics, the afterglows, the lilac tree. The spittle-wet sleeve around the snowdrop-bouquet has dried, says the pianist, the pianist's shirt-cuff—we sat across from each other in silence, the pianist says to me, eavesdropped on new verses of Ferdinand Schmatz, while the composer hands me *an open-faced sandwich* (a filth sandwich) across the table, which I fold together. The composer leaves the room and climbs into the hallway window in order to plunge himself into the deep, I grab him by the legs, pull him back—the pianist says, *played the piano inly today etc.* this *blood-colony* = blood-culture is like a l. forest, young forest growing slowly, so says the composer, the doctors

te auf Klavier innig gespielt usw. diese *Blutkolonie* = Blutkultur
ist wie 1 kl. Wald, Jungwald der langsam wächst, so der Komponist, die Ärzte vermuten, dieser Befund am Wochenanfang,
so 1 Blut Orgie, so 1 Blutorgel, sieh wie aus den Orgelpfeifen
die Blutstropfen wie Tränen, ich sah zu, so der Komponist, wie
die Pianistin am PALMSONNTAG die Palmzweige mit Weih-
wasser bestrich, eigentlich streichelte, es jagte mir die Tränen.

Die Frühjahrsstürme so heftig dasz er, der Komponist, die
Mähne der Rösser hüllte in karierte Decke, die Mähne der
Rösser streichelte, dasz er die Tasten risz und zerrisz, dasz er
den 4.Finger der rechten Hand *(Ringfinger)* hochrisz und
hochbäumte und hochband an der Decke des Arbeitszimmers
dasz es ihn schmerzte, weil nämlich der 4.Finger *(Ringfinger)*
der rechten Hand, der die Melodie übernahm nicht deutlich
genug anschlug etc. Nach der Pianistin betrat die Hündin das
Zimmer, mit fliegendem Atem. Die Glaubwürdigkeit eines
Kunstwerks, so der Komponist, ist nicht immer zu gründen
auf reichlichem Tränenvergieszen bis heran an die Pelzstola,
da überholte mich jemand mit einem Nerzcape mitten im 1.
Hauch des neuen Frühlings ich meine Frühlingserschrecken,
plötzlich erschraken wir alle weil die Explosion des Frühlings,
sein Weben und Erbeben und dasz die Sträucher und Bäume =
Haine über Nacht übergeworfen hatten diesen FLOR lichtgrün
und Schleier, wenngleich noch nicht tatsächlich wahrnehm-
bar, noch 1 Geheimnis nicht wahr. Diese winzigen lichtgrünen
Blättchen, klebrigen Knospen der Kastanienbäume, während
die Pianistin verkündet ANGST und SEXUALITÄT beherrschen
die Welt usw. »die Luft ist voll von unseren Schreien« (Beckett) *es düstert mich*, so die Pianistin, wenn ich an die Leiden des
Komponisten denke, gestern der Mond in seinem schwarzen
Hemd, in seinem zunehmenden Wahn, sasz dann auf seinem
Mäntelchen (Hündchen), in seinem fliegenden Garten, über
dem Haupt: Hänfling der aufschwirrt, Elevation des Komponisten, Elevation des Monds, Aprilwind und Gala, sein schmaler

surmise, this result at the beginning of the week, such a blood orgy, such a blood-organ, see how out of the organ pipes the drops of blood like tears, I saw, so says the composer, how the pianist on PALM SUNDAY brushed, actually stroked, the palm branches with holy water, tears chasing from me.

The vernal storms so severe that he, the composer, draped the steeds' manes in checkered blanket, stroked the steeds' manes, that he tore and tore apart the keys, that he tore up reared up and tied up the right hand's 4th finger *(ring finger)* to the ceiling of the workroom that it pained him, because namely the right hand's 4th finger *(ring finger)*, which took over the melody was not striking it clearly enough etc. After the pianist the female dog entered the room, with soaring breath. The credibility of an art work, so says the composer, isn't always to be founded upon ample tears shed right on up to the fur-stole, there someone with a mink cape overtook me amid the 1st waft of the new spring I mean startling of spring, suddenly all of us startled because the explosion of spring, its weave and trembling and that the shrubs and trees = grove had thrown over this VELUM overnight lightgreen and veil, albeit still not really perceivable, still a secret isn't it. These tiny lightgreen leaflets, sticky buds of the chestnut trees, while the pianist proclaims FEAR and SEXUALITY rule the world etc. »the air is full of our cries« (Beckett) *it glooms me*, so says the pianist, when I think of the pianist's sorrows, yesterday the moon in its black shirt, in its growing delirium, then sat on its coatlet (doglet), in its flying garden, overhead : linnet that whirred up, elevation of the composer, elevation of the moon, April-wind and gala, its narrow foot in butterfly white, the hollyhocks = mallows at the city's edge, my half-body says to the composer, I see your floating hat your panicked mouth, *puffy-sleeved* in the garden in the garbling coos, I see you all huddled up unclothed, in the curled cyme-bush, with soughing rubber apron, *in your*

Fusz in Schmetterlingsweisz, die Pappelrosen = Malven am Stadtrand, mein Halbkörper sagt zum Komponisten, ich sehe deine schwebende Mütze deinen panischen Mund, *puffärmelig* im Garten im Gurren, ich sehe dich zusammengekauert unbekleidet, im Wickelbusch, mit sausender Gummischürze, *in deiner Verschworenheit* dieser Purpurfrühling, der Fuji, dahinter das blutende Abendrot, so die Pianistin, die Pianistin habe weite Konzertreisen unternommen während der Komponist in der Nervenklinik von Endenich. Er habe unablässig Noten aufgeschrieben : diese Aufzeichnungen seien jedoch verschollen – man habe ihn ohne Erfolg u.a. mit Chinin behandelt, die amerikan. Germanistin Lisa K. fragte mich, so die Pianistin, was empfinden Sie als »häszliche Schönheit von Amerika«, die Pianistin sei als *Windsbraut* mit nach hinten *geblasenen* Haaren (Haarschöpfen) an der Straszenkreuzung gestanden und habe mit dem Komponisten geflüstert, mit dieser Flamme in den Haaren etc. Hatte Beutel schweres Herz in der Nacht, so der Komponist, muszte einnehmen ½ Tablette Cenipres hatte UNTERPFAND hatte Empathie für kl. alte *waagrechte* Frau welche über die trasze *gekrochen* welche an Morbus Bechterew gelitten, welche sich nicht mehr habe aufrichten können der naive Maler Henri Rousseau, genannt »der Zöllner« habe sich mit violetten Schlangen umgeben um arbeiten zu können, so der Komponist mein Halbkörper sagt zum Komponisten, lege dir 2 jg.Freunde bei dasz du erinnert wirst an dein baldiges *Fuszwallen* (mit schönen Pedaleffekten). Während die vertrocknete Aprikose auf schwarzem Steingutteller.

In meinem kindlichen Geist schien es mir, wir saszen am linken Ufer der Traun und sahen der Strömung zu, so die Pianistin, blickten auch zum anderen Ufer sahen uns selbst im kl. gelben Talbot und manövrierend, einem in rasendem Tempo uns entgegenkommenden Wagen im letzten Augenblick ausweichend, *wie die Täler blitzten.*

Die Quellchen und Täubchen, Sputum und Spuren des Gefühls einer Geistigkeit des Komponisten, lange die Nieder-

conspiring this crimsonspring, Mt. Fuji, off behind it the bleeding afterglow, so says the pianist, the said pianist having embarked on many concert trips while the composer in the psychiatric clinic of Endenich. That he'd written down notes incessantly : these notations however have vanished—he was treated unsuccessfully with quinine among other treatments, the American Germanist Lisa K. asked me, so says the pianist, what do you feel to be the »hideous beauty of America«, that the pianist as *bride of the wind* was standing at the intersection with back-*blown* hair (shocks of hair) and was whispering with the composer, with this flame in her hair etc. Had bags heavy heart in the night, so says the composer, had to imbibe ½ tablet of Cenipres had PLEDGED felt empathy for l. old *levelled* woman who had *crawled* over the street who had suffered from Morbus Bechterew, who was unable to stand up straight the naïve painter Henri Rousseau, known as »the Taxman« had surrounded himself with violet snakes in order to work, so says the composer my half-body says to the composer, add 2 yg. friends to your side that you will be reminded of your imminent *foot-roiling* (with beautiful pedal-effects). While the dried-up apricot on the black earthenware plate.

To my childlike mind it seemed to me, we were sitting on the left riverbank of the Traun and watching the current, so says the pianist, gazed across to the other side too we saw ourselves in the l. yellow Talbot and maneuvering, at the very last instant swerving away from a car coming toward us at racing speed, *as the valleys flashed.*

The sourcelets and dovelets, sputum and spoors of feeling of the composer's esprit, long the confinement, long having walked up and down the Naschmarkt, later hurried into the »Drechsler«, drank wine and pear juice, sat in the corner with the pianist, glance upon Spanish appearing garlands and

kunft, lange den Naschmarkt aufund abgegangen, später ins »Drechsler« geeilt, Wein getrunken und Birnensaft, in der Ecke gesessen mit der Pianistin, Blick auf spanisch anmutende Girlanden und Erkerplätzchen von gegenüber, und neben den neuen lichtgrünen Ästchen das dünne bräunliche Blätter-rauschen da der Wind noch nicht altes Laub *hinweggeblasen*, die Pianistin mit der *weggeblasenen* Frisur dasz ihre Stirn sich entblöszte was ihr ein tobendes tollkühnes Aussehen verlieh – im Hintergrund der moribunde Komponist seitwärts, auf seinem Soffa, aufschreibend fieberhaft seine stammelnden Par-tituren, uns nicht beachtend in seinem Frühlings Wahn, und was das »Drechsler« angeht hatten wir es zuletzt im tiefen Schneetreiben besucht, damals bei rauchendem glosendem Ofen, *Geschmauche*, etc., was das »Drechsler« angehe, so die Pianistin, jetzt im 1. Fahnenschwenken des Lenzes, sehe man die spanisch anmutende *Laube* von gegenüber : das brüchige *Laub* welches noch nicht vom Rasen des Lenzwindes *weggebla-sen* wo jg. Käfer und Spinnen im Osten, was das in der Nische Sitzen im »Drechsler« angehe, so die Pianistin, und den PA-PIER AUSRISZ meines Herzens, so die Pianistin, wenn ich an den hinscheidenden Komponisten denke, welcher den Wein schlürfend von meinem Finger : lag meist entblöszt (»cher«), seeliges Hinterhaupt, wundliegen : Absterbenmachen durch Aufliegen Durchliegen, wehmütiges Lied usw. etwa Schlamm in den Augen, meine verströmenden Füsze, so der Komponist, da so Zungen am Horizont, auf Nessel gemalt, und, was ihr Kla-vierspiel angeht, so der Komponist, soll wieder klavierspielen für mich, einen Chopin, einen Brahms, einen Bach, ein Hirten-stück etwa, etwas von mir, die »symphonischen Etüden«, op.13, z. B., in den höchsten Coloraturen. Die gemurmelten Ausrufe, »hallo« im Telefon, das sagte er, so meldete er sich oder er sagte seinen vollständigen Namen, manchmal verbeug-te er sich mit dem Hörer am linken Ohr das besser hören kon-nte als das rechte (wenn er sich vorstellte, meldete), überhaupt

orioles from across the way, and alongside the new lightgreen branchlets the thin brownish rustling of leaves since the wind not yet having *blown-off-and-away* old foliage, the pianist with the blown-off haircut that her forehead bared itself which lent her a romping look of daring—in the background the moribund composer sidelong, on his sofa, writing his stammering scores down, not observing us in his springtime frenzy, and as what concerns »Café Drechsler« we had last visited it among deep drifts of snow, that time whilst smoking glimmering stove, *puffing away*, etc., as what concerns the »Drechsler«, so says the pianist, now in the 1st flag-wavings of springtide, if 1 sees the Spanish appearing *arbor* from across the way : the brittle *foliage* that hasn't yet been *blown-away* from the turf of the springtide-wind where yg.beetles and spiders in the east, as what concerns the sitting in the alcove at the »Drechsler«, so says the pianist, and the PAPER CUTOUT of my heart, so says the pianist, when I think of the composer passing on, the 1 sipping wine from my finger : lay mostly exposed (»cher«), blessed back of the head, bedsores : necrosis from lying abed pressure sores, wistful song etc. maybe mud in the eyes, my feet streaming away, so says the composer, there sort of tongues on the horizon, painted-on nettles, and, as what concerns her piano playing, so says the composer, should play piano for myself again, a Chopin, a Brahms, a Bach, a pastoral piece perhaps, something of my own, the »symphonic etudes«, op.13, e.g., in the highest coloratures. The murmured exclamations, »hello« into the phone, that's what he said, so he answered or he said his full name, sometimes he bent forward with the receiver to the left ear that could hear better than the right 1 (when he introduced himself, answered), indeed his facial features were in liveliest motion while he phoned, »hello« *the scent of speech, Jacques Derrida—*

waren seine Gesichtszüge in lebhaftester Bewegung während er telefonierte, »hallo« *der Duft einer Rede, Jacques Derrida* –

sie blieb in der Passage des *Naschmarkts* stehen und rief in ihrem Manschetten Traum »meditativ«, »kontemplativ«, »pejorativ«, worauf der Komponist sprach, »wo bist du?«, möchte lieber Geist sein als Fleisch, so die Pianistin, *das handgemalte Ja* = Prozession einer Biographie, usw. 1 Frage z. B. an einen anderen, worauf sogleich die ÜBERSTÜRZTE Antwort folgt, bevor der Befragte überlegen kann was er antworten könne. Habe heute viel grammophoniert, so die Pianistin, Werke von Schumann, Brahms, Chopin und Bach, und hatte so ein Röckchen = blaues Faltenröckchen an, damals mit 8, neben dem Seerosenteich in der Privatschule, so die Pianistin, sollte auf dem Schulklavier etwas von Chopin spielen, zitterte so und atemlos dasz ich nicht spielen konnte wofür ich mich schämte, »my mountain flower«, so der Komponist zur Pianistin. Möchte wieder ins »Drechsler« und lange aus dem groszen Fenster *starren* auf die Blumen Momente von gegenüber die kl. Erker staubigen alten Laubs. (»do it in the bath«, Joyce/Derrida), Knospe des Fleisches, so der Komponist, und wie sich immer der Staub in der Nabelgrube ansammelt, nicht wahr, ach ich, dieses elektrische Ich, so der Komponist, die Tasten schlagend, haben wir uns nicht immerzu mit unserer verrückten Liebe angesteckt, so der Komponist (salutierend) – dasz ich mich *letzten Endes* VERDUFTE mit den 1. Magnolien dieses Frühlings, so der Komponist, auf dem offenen Soffa sich wälzend was die Aussparung von Personen auf einem Gruppenfoto (Familienfoto) angeht, gibt es auf einem bestimmten Foto, das eine gröszere Familiengruppe abbildet, nur noch eine Person die am Leben ist, und auch diese Person die als etwa 3-jähriges Mädchen abgebildet ist steht am Rande des Grabes, hinfällig, dement, in skandalöser Weise vergrämt – so dasz es sie verlangt, unter Tränen, sich zuzurufen : KRÜPPEL !, RUINE ! (siehe Jacques Derrida)

she stood still in the passageway of the *Naschmarkt* and shouted in her sleeve dream »meditative«, »contemplative«, »pejorative«, upon which the composer spoke, »where are you?«, would rather be spirit than flesh, so says the pianist, *the hand-painted YES* = cavalcade of a biography, etc. a question e.g. for an other, upon which the HEADLONG answer follows, before the 1 questioned can consider how 1 could answer. Gramophoned a lot today, so says the pianist, works by Schumann, Brahms, Chopin and Bach, and had some sort of short skirt = short blue pleated skirt on, that time when 8, beside the lily pond at private school, so says the pianist, was supposed to play something by Chopin on the school piano, trembled so and breathless that I couldn't play for which I felt ashamed, »*my mountain flower*«, so says the composer to the pianist. Would like to go back to »Café Drechsler« and *stare* long out the big window upon the flowers moments from across the way the l. oriel of dusty old foliage. (»*do it in the bath*«, Joyce/Derrida), sprout of the flesh, so says the composer, and how dust always collects in the navel pit, isn't it so, this electric I, so says the composer, striking the keys, have we not infected ourselves to no end with our crazed love, so says the composer (saluting)—that *at the last* I EVAPORATE with this spring's 1st magnolias, so says the composer, throwing himself onto the open sofa as what concerns the blank spaces of persons on a group photo (family photo), there's a certain photo, it depicts a larger family group, only 1 person of which is still living, and this person too who's depicted at about 3 years old also stands at the grave's edge, infirm, demented, careworn in scandalous fashion—so that she's compelled among tears to call out to herself : CRIPPLE!, WRECK! (see Jacques Derrida)

we then went into the »Drechsler« and I *stared* into the open space into the passageways of the Naschmarkt in which the thronging = *jostling* of humans and the glinting springday de-

wir gingen dann ins »Drechsler« und ich *starrte* ins Freie in die Passagen des Naschmarkts in welchen das Gedränge = *Geschiebe* der Menschen und der glänzende Frühlingstag sie unendlich verschlang, mit den kl. Primadonnen im österlichen Himmel etc.

Ich weinte viel, so die Pianistin und las wieder in Jacques Derridas »Ulysses Grammophon« während der Komponist ein Telefongespräch mit Francis Ponge führte und ihm innig seine neue Komposition über das Telefon vorspielte, dabei weinte : hingebungsvoll dem eigenen Ende *entgegengeschlachtet* wie jene tote schwarze Katze mit glänzendem Fell im Hausflur mit aufgesperrtem Mund, herzzerreiszenden Zähnchen, geschlossenen Augen und gestreckten Gliedmaszen, 1 erschütternde Figur. Wohin sie sich vermutlich mit letzter Kraft GESCHLEPPT bevor der Geist sie verliesz, aus ihrem offenen Mund 1 stummer Schrei nämlich *Todes Schleim* usw.

1 zusammenhangloses Blitzen, so der Komponist, die Komposition die mir *geisterte*, dasz mir die Trübnisse die Dunkelrosen nämlich, der Nacht, so mit ausgebüschelten Flügeln und Armen wie die Eidechse *starrt*, auf dem sonnenbeschienenen Stein ruhend (oder Knochen), mitten in ihrer Wildnis : starrend lange starrend ins Gebüsch an ihrer Seite = Schulter, lange starrend ohne Bewegung, aber dann plötzlich den schönen Kopf zur Seite *reiszend* : 1 blitzender Ruck zur Seite 1 zerrissener Reflex : so die Gedanken Empfindungen zerrissen gerissen zur Seite gerissen, so der Komponist auf dem offenen Soffa, mein erschaudernder Wahn meine erschaudernde Wildnis im Schädel, das entblöszte Veilchen auf dem Friedhof, so die Pianistin, die Bougainvilles die ich dem Komponisten in die Anstalt mitgebracht hatte, fühlten sich an wie künstliche Blumen, knisternd knitternd und raschelnd, was für 1 Zynismus, so der Komponist, *ich lasse die Schmerzen zu*, also auf die Äuszerungen meines Körpers und Geistes nicht achtend, nämlich auf die Gestrandetheit meines Geschlechts usw., knüllte die Stirn, meine Geschlechtskrankheit ..

voured them endlessly, with the l. prima donnas in the easterly
sky etc.

I cried lots, so says the pianist and read Jacques Derrida's » Ulysses
Gramophone « while the composer carried on a phone con-
versation with Francis Ponge and played him his newest composition INLY over the phone, whilst crying : devotedly
slaughtered toward l's own end as that dead black cat with
shiny fur and mouth agape in the entranceway, heartrending
tiny teeth, closed eyes and stretched limbs, 1 unsettling figure.
Where it had presumably DRAGGED itself to with its last ounce
of strength before its spirit departed, from its mouth a mute cry
namely *phlegm of death* etc.

1 disjointed lightning, so says the composer, the composition
which *haunted* me, that sorrows to me the dark roses namely,
of the night, so with unbundled wings and arms how the lizard
stares, resting on the sunlit stone (or bone), in the midst of its
wilderness : staring long staring into the bushes alongside it
= shoulder, staring long without moving, but then suddenly
snapping its handsome head to the side : 1 flashing jerk to the
side 1 snapped reflex : so the thoughts sensations snapped tore
torn to the side, so says the composer on the open sofa, my
shuddering delirium my shuddering wilderness in the skull,
the exposed violet at the graveyard, so says the pianist, the
bougainvillea that I had brought with me to the institution for
the composer, felt like artificial flowers, crinkling creasing and
rustling, what cynicism, so says the composer, I admit the pain,
i.e. not attending to the pronouncements of my body and mind,
that is, to the strandedness of my generation etc., furrowed the
brow, my genital disease ..

the composer *tip-toeing* around and nocturnally, the grasses
wet in the garden, the 1st violets : plucked a bouquetlet, wound
wet sleeve around it, enquired after his state of being with my
eyes, so says the pianist, requested new sleeves and springtime

der Komponist *tip-toeing* umher und nächtens, die Gräser feucht im Garten, die 1.Veilchen : pflückte ein Sträuszchen, umwand es mit feuchter Manschette, fragte ihn mit meinen Augen nach seinem Befinden, so die Pianistin, bat um neue Manschetten und Frühjahrsgewand, da Klamotten vom Vorjahr nicht auffindbar, usw., geht mit gefalteten Händen im Garten zwischen den Büschen umher, Stoszgebete, Flüche ausstoszend, faselte, ist verstimmt, raschelten Musikalien : Notenpapier und Paganini, Harnverhalten, Schmerz im Scheitel, Veilchen ihre Farbe *gebüszt* hatten, bis gepflückte Veilchen ihre Farbe gebüszt hatten, *das grosze Siebengebirge davor.*

In Filzschuhen. Wie er erzählt, auf welchen Bergen er gewesen sei dasz er in Düsseldorf die Blumen GEPFLEGT, die Pianistin wünscht ihm allerlei Kleinigkeiten (zu senden) Blumen und Cigarren z. B. Fertigschreibend Variationen über ein Thema das ihm »Engel als Grusz von Mendelssohn und Schubert« hören lieszen, *vielleicht 1 Nervenstechen*, nicht wahr, als wir saszen und hockten im Götterbaum im Erlenbaum, so der Komponist, im Totenköpfchen im Schnee –

ach! die Waage zu finden zwischen den Lustgärten der Sprache und den Schluchten der Sprache oder Schluchzen der Sprache auch Ginsterwald. In der Brotlade das verschimmelte Brot, und fallen ihm die Tabletten aus der Hand während er sie zum Mund führt er gräbt dann in dem Gewand = Gewandung (Gerundium) des Vorfrühlings in grüngefalteter Bäume Erleuchtung, 1 Lustigkeit, Façon einer Lustigkeit, wie ROBOTER sprechen, »ich habe meine Trompete verloren«, so der Komponist, »es geht darum, Gefühlsbereiche zu entwerfen zu erfinden, Kritzeleien zu entwerfen, wilde Telefone, Albträume, elastische Scharniere – alle haben sie gelacht, und in hl. Heiterkeit sind die Generationen dahingesunken, eigentlich alles zum Lachen dieser Kitzel des Lebens, und so nah dem Weinen verbunden, die Schründe die Zirben im Flockentaumel des Vorfrühlings, usw.«

garment, since last year's clothes not to be found, etc., walks around the garden between the bushes with hands folded, devout ejaculations, ejecting curses, blathered out of tune, rustled sheet music : scoring paper and Paganini, urinary retention, pain in the part, violets had *atoned* their color, until plucked violets had atoned their color, *the imposing Sieben mountains before them.*

In felt shoes. How he tells it, atop which mountains he's been that in Düsseldorf he CARED for the flowers, all sorts of odds and ends the pianist wishes (to send) for him flowers and cigars e.g.

Finishing writing variations on a theme that would allow him to hear » angel as a greeting from Mendelssohn and Schubert «, *a throbbing nerve perhaps,* isnt't it, as we sat and crouched in the tree of heaven in the alder tree, so says the composer, in death's headlet in the snow—

ach! to find the scale balanced between the pleasure gardens of language and the gorges of language or sobbing of language genista forest too. In the bread drawer the moldy bread, and were the tablets to fall out of his hand while he raises them to the mouth he then digs in his garment = garb (gerund) of the early-spring in green-folded trees illumination, a humorousness, mode of a humorousness, how ROBOTS speak, »I lost my trumpet«, so says the composer, »it's a matter of drafting of drawing up realms of feeling, of drafting jots and scribbles, wild telephones, nightmares, elastic hinges—all of them were laughing, and in holy cheerfulness the generations have sunk away beyond, actually all of it laughable this tickle of life, and so closely connected to crying, the crevasses the pines in the flake-frenzy of early-spring, etc.«

»At the end of the sheet (of the Satan) when we *played footsie*«, so says the pianist. As what concerns this black cat, she possessed

»Am Ende der Seite (des Satans) wenn wir *füszelten*«, so die Pianistin. Was diese tote schwarze Katze angeht, besasz sie eine grosze Schönheit, ihr Fell glänzte, ihre Erscheinung schien ein Geheimnis zu hüten, die Gliedmaszen in einer langen Sehnsucht hingestreckt, ich habe Varese gehört, die Sensation der Wortfolgen, das Vibrieren der Veilchen im Garten, habe die Sitten Schrift gelesen, den Lerchenspiegel gesehen, mir träumt, das Knarren meiner Schuhe auf den Bohlenbrettern hatte den Vortrag der Pianistin gestört, 1 Bild von Andreas Grunert trug den Titel, »die Haare Gottes auf dem Bretterboden«, Acryl auf Nessel, diese plötzliche Ärztin, so der Komponist, 1 Wassertropfen aus dem Himmel fällt, 1 Federchen aus Stoff und Watte und viel Gerümpel, die Sprache der Vögel und mystische Brust.

Er habe dann noch die ganze Nacht phantasiert und mit offenen Haaren, aufgeschlagenen Blicken, später hätten ihm die Engel Schlaf versprochen er sei *in die Exaltation geraten dasz es ihm von der Stirne troff,* während, der Mond Äther ganz rein und klar, ganz in der Nacht seines Zimmers die Nachtigallen schlagen hören, er sagte dann, man hüte sich als Künstler den Zusammenhang mit der Gesellschaft zu verlieren sonst geht man unter wie ich, nicht wahr, die Fontanelle ist 1 Löckchen, 1 weiszes Löckchen oder HANDSCHUH im Vorraum zusammengeknüllt, man musz es empfinden, man musz die Sprache empfinden, hier und da ein Gewicht darauflegen oder wegnehmen wie Apothekerwaage, so musz es stimmen, so musz es *tönen,* das Panorama meines ganzen Lebens vor mir ausgebreitet, wie *ovaler,* Olivengarten, von schönen Welten träumen, so der Komponist, sehe den Mt. Blanc, usw.

Was die Katze angeht, so die Pianistin, intensive Katzen Gold Jahre mit *Robert,* was den Tod dieser schwarzen Katze angeht : die Verherrlichung einer Einsamkeit, *1 Art Reseda.* Der Komponist schreibt in ein Buch das geöffnet auf seinen Knien liegt, während die Pianistin seine schwarze Mütze und Handschuhe, und er den Feldweg zum Rhein in Begleitung seiner Aufseh-

great beauty, her fur shone, her appearance seemed to guard a secret, the extremities outstretched in elongate yearning, I listened to Varese, the sensation of word sequences, the vibrations of the violets in the garden, read the moral weekly, saw the lark's mirror, me dreams, the creaking of my shoes on the floor planks had disturbed the pianist's presentation, 1 painting by Andreas Grunert bore the title, »the hairs of God on the floorboards«, acrylic on nettle, this sudden doctor, so says the composer, 1 waterdrop out of the sky falls, 1 featherlet of fabric and wadding and much rummage, the language of birds and mystical breast.

He then went on to fantasize all night and with loose hair, wide-open gazes, the angels promised him sleep later he was *caught up in the exaltation that it dripped from his brow*, meanwhile, the moon ether wholly pure and clear, wholly in the night of his room hearing the nightingales trilling, he then said, 1 must be on 1's guard as an artist to keep from losing the connection to society otherwise 1 goes under like me, isn't it so, the fontanelle is 1 ringlet, 1 white ringlet or GLOVE bunched up in the entry-room, 1 has to feel it, 1 has to feel language, to lay on or take off 1 weight here and there like pharmacist scale, so it must sound, so tuned, the panorama of my whole life spread out before me, as *oval*, olive garden, to dream of beautiful worlds, so says the composer, see Mt. Blanc, etc.

As what concerns the cat, so says the pianist, intensive cats golden years with *Robert*, as what concerns this black cat's death : the extolling of a loneliness, *1 kind of reseda*. The composer writes in a book that lies open on his knees, while the pianist his black hat and gloves, and he the field-path to the Rhine accompanied by his supervisors namely within the surroundings of the resedas, he pecked with metal grabber-arm from the floor what was there shaken to pieces, scraplets sleeves

er nämlich im Umkreis der Reseden, er pickte mit metallen-
em *Greifarm* vom Fuszboden was da auseinandergeschüttelt,
Zettelchen Manschetten Brotkrümel – weil er sich nicht mehr
bücken konnte oder wollte, weil 1 Ausschüttung seiner selbst
bevorstand, so die Pianistin.

Was die Fotografie dieser Ringelnatter unter der Gieszkanne in
Angelika Kaufmanns Garten angeht, wagte es diese nicht, die
Gieszkanne hochzuheben nämlich das scheue Tier aufzuzu-
schrecken, nicht wahr, ähnlich erging es ihr mit der Fotografie
der toten Katze im Hausflur welche hingegeben an ihre *Be-
grenzung* über das glänzende Fell – heute gebunden, mit rötli-
chem Schleim – schon war das Grab bewachsen, und wenig
Wochen und Vogel Temperatur und die innerlichsten Land-
schaften, in Unterkunft der Reseden. So wurde die Nacht zum
Tag, er sasz oft bis in die Morgenstunden über seinen Noten-
heften und es strömte aus seinem Kopf, in seinen nervösen
Aufzeichnungen : leidenden Variationen, auch stellten sich
Raserei und heftige Krampfanfälle ein, recht mitteilsam Hals-
tuch, »Gesänge von Maria Stuart«, im Lichthof Tauben und
russ.Saatkrähen wie laut sprechend mit Echo, dasz man an böse
Geister denken müsse (»Geistervariationen«, ohne Opuszahl,
Es-Dur). Unsere Kinder als Kügelchen zu sehen, im Tal, so
die Pianistin zu Robert, (und jetzt würd' es schon ganz jour-
nalistisch solch übler Stil), es gebe 47 Gründe, in der Nacht zu
schwitzen, so der Arzt, nachdem der Komponist vorbringt, er
fürchte lungenkrank zu sein

Vorhautbändchen des Penis gebissen, von Narzissen, so der
Komponist, bin Fusz Fetischist, wie Max Bense, mache Beis-
chlafkreuzchen ins Tagebuch, küsse die Füsze der Pianistin,
mit dem Pelzchen aller Nacht, zuweilen summend auf dem Soffa, lispelnd, Aloe groszer Adler über dem Bett – 1 Verdikt 1
Gleichgewicht : Glöckchen der Welt ergibt sich aus dem Wag-
nis, die Schriften eines unbekannten Dichters zu lesen, so der

bread crumbs—because 1 outpouring of his very self awaited, so says the pianist.

As what concerns the photograph of this ring snake under the watering can in Angelika Kaufmann's garden, the latter did not dare lift up the watering can namely to startle the shy animal, isn't it so, she fared similarly with the photograph of the dead cat in the entranceway which surrendered to its boundary over the shiny fur—bound today, with reddish phlegm—already the grave was overgrown, and few weeks and bird temperature and the inmost landscapes, in shelter of the resedas. So night became day, he often sat over his manuscript notebooks until deep into the morning hours and it streamed from his head, in his nervous notations : suffering variations, frenzy and fits of convulsion came on too, rather forthcoming neckcloth, »Songs of Maria Stuart«, in the atrium pigeons and rooks as if speaking aloud with an echo, that 1 thought of evil spirits (»ghost variations«, without opus number, e-flat major). To see our children as globules, in the valley, so says the pianist to Robert, (and now it was even getting quite journalistic such horrid style), there are 47 reasons, to sweat at night, so says the doctor, after the composer brings up being afraid that he had contracted lung disease

Ridged band of the penis stung, by daffodils, so says the composer, I'm a foot fetishist, like Max Bense, make coitus-checkmarks in my diary, kiss the feet of the pianist, *with the furlet of every night*, at times humming on the sofa, lisping, aloe large eagle over the bed—1 verdict 1 balance : tiny bell of the world arises from the risk, to read the writings of an unknown poet, so says the composer, *the environmemory in the hair,* so says the composer, heaving himself onto the open sofa while inside in her brassierlet, the pianist's *brassierlet* all filled with cellulose and wadding i.e. pinned inside her brassierlet : filled

Komponist, *das Umweltgedächtnis in den Haaren*, so der Komponist, sich auf dem offenen Soffa wälzend während innen in ihrem *Busenkleid*, der Pianistin Busenkleidchen alles mit Zellulose und Watte gefüllt also innen in ihrem Busenkleidchen festgesteckt : angefüllt ausgestopft dasz der Busen üppiger erscheine – wie ältere Männer Watte Zellulose in ihre Hose, ich meine innen in ihrer Hose, etc.

So viele Jahre *zurückblätternd* ins Café Museum in der *lounge*, sehr angefüllt und angestopft mit Emotionen, an *ihn* lehnend, schweigend, später zur Telefonkabine, Mutter anrufend, zurückkehrend zu *ihm* in die Loge (schwarzes Leder knautschiges Leder), mich an *ihn* himmelnd, murmelnd, er mir schweigend, zu mir schweigend, dasz meine Tränen in flutender Wehmut, in groszer Innigkeit zu seiner Seelenweisheit und er seinen Arm um meine Schulter und mich anblickend mit grauen Augenbällen, wie Blumen, graublauen Augenbällen, nämlich die Cigarillos, beedies, duftende Pfeife schmauchend, »möchte wieder mit dir ins ›Drechsler‹ «, so die Pianistin zu Robert, schwarzen Bindfaden statt Lesezeichen eingelegt zwischen die Seiten des Buches, was den schwarzen Bindfaden in meinem Bett/auf dem offenen Soffa angeht, so der Komponist, ist es die Nabelschnur die mich immer noch, nach so vielen Jahren, mit meiner Mutter verbindet und »*was mir den ganzen Rest stibitzt*« (Jean Genet), was mich aufgewühlt hat, bin *Chimäre*, so der Komponist, lange blieb ich am Rand hocken, 1 (mein) winziges hartes Exkrement auf dem Fliesenboden des Abtritts wie Kot von Geiszen, vom harten Licht des Abtritts angestrahlt, Mutters Lieblingspflanze = die Wedel der Baumfarne, strich sie durch Forst, Mutter pflanzte sich Wedel der Baumfarne ins milde Augenlicht, war angewurzelt wie 1 Pflanze –

die Tablette, die er sich zum Munde führen wollte, entglitt seiner Hand, was das Verschwinden/Verlöschen von Tabletten in seinen Gewändern angeht beim vergeblichen Versuch, die Tablette zum Munde zu führen, allzu Glorie, suchte er in

up stuffed in that the breast would appear more ample—like older men wadding cellulose in their pants, I mean on the inside of their pants, etc.

So many years *turning pages back* into the Café Museum in the lounge, pretty jam-full and jam-packed with emotions, leaning on *him*, in silence, to the phone booth later, calling Mother, returning to *him* in the loge (black leather crumpled leather), me making eyes at *him*, mumbling, in silence for me, in silence to me, that my tears with brimming wistfulness, in great intimacy with his soul-wisdom and he his arm around my shoulder and gazing at me with gray eyeballs, like flowers, blue-gray eyeballs, namely the cigarillos, beedies, fragrant pipe puffing away, »would like to go to the ›Drechsler‹ with you again«, so says the pianist to Robert, black packthread instead of bookmark inlaid between the pages of the book, as what concerns the black packthread in my bed/on the open sofa, so says the composer, it's the umbilical cord that even still, after so many years, connects me to my mother and »*what swipes me of all the rest*« (Jean Genet), what churned me up, am *chimera*, so says the composer, I stayed on the edge squatting for a long time, 1 (my) minuscule hard excrement on the tile floor of the privy like dung of nanny goats, beamed at by the hard light of the privy, Mother's beloved plant = fronds of tree fern, happening to cross through forest, Mother planted fronds of tree fern in the mild eye's light, was rooted as 1 plant —

the tablet, which he had wanted to guide to his mouth, slipped from his hand, as what concerns the evanescence/vanishments of tablets in his garments, whilst the vain effort, of guiding the tablet to the mouth, all too glory, he searched in the folds of his garment and perceived *this unclean spot* : the shrill echo of the corpse-body's threads, threads, as if the tablets were perhaps in the folds of his *corps-of-Khirgizes* and seized deep-freezed metamorphosized by them —

den Falten seines Gewandes und nahm wahr *diese unreine Stelle*
: den schrillen Widerhall der *Leibesfäden*, als ob die Tabletten
etwa in die Falten seiner Leibeskirgisen und von diesen einge-
fangen eingefroren verwandelt worden wären –

ich vergesse was ich gelesen habe ich vergesse was ich geschrie-
ben habe was ich gesprochen habe, so der Komponist, aus dem
Wort »Schmerzen« werden ZOFEN weil ich schwärme von
Jean Genet, wenn ich dahin bin schluchzet die Nachtigall oder
Ulme, so der Komponist, mein zerrüttetes Hörvermögen, so
der Komponist, wenn Clara ruft, hörst du den Vogelruf, ich
kann den Vogelruf vor dem Fenster nicht hören, ich lege meine
lauschend gekrümmte Hand an mein rechtes Ohr damit sie
1 Trichter sei, 1 Hörrohr, oder *irgendwas Irisches*, 1 wallen-
de Sphäre, Metropole, irgend 1 Greifarm irgend Blüten und
Brüder in Beeten etc.

was die in die Faltentiefe der Gewänder sinkenden Tabletten
angeht, so der Komponist, scheinen sie begleitet von den Klän-
gen der Wesendoncklieder, dem Rauschen der Baumkronen
im Garten, den wie Ärmchen ausgespannten Knospen der
Kastanientriebe in eine Vase

NÄMLICH DIE SCHNUTE, jener Gefühls-, Geschmacks-,
Geruchs-Erweckung vom pausenlosen Klopfen der Tröpf-
chen aus der Wasserleitung ins halbvolle Becken in welchem
der Strausz Anemonen : noch zusammengebunden, die Stengel mit nassem Zeitungspapier umwickelt, dieser Strausz zerrissener Blütenblätter, zart gefranst, in den Farben rot rosa
orange, weil ich zu müde war, den Strausz in die Bodenvase :
die Bodenvase mit Wasser anzufüllen dann den Strausz zu *arrangieren* während das *Gewand* eines Blumenzustandes einer
Vorstellung von Schokolade von Brocken alten Gebäcks in
einem Papiersack, indem sie, die Pianistin, die Tasten schlug
– also war es spätnachts da die Pianistin auf ihrem niedrigen
Klavierstuhl vornübergeneigt, beinahe den Boden berührend

I forget what I've read I forget what I've written what I've said, so says the composer, from the word »pains« become MAIDS because I gush over Jean Genet, when I'm dashed off sobs the nightingale or elm, so says the composer, my shattered hearing, so says the composer, when Clara calls, you hear the bird call, I can't hear the bird call at the window, I set my hearkening bent hand to my right ear so that it's 1 speculum, 1 hearing rod, or *anything Earse*, 1 seething sphere, metropolis, any 1 grabber-arm any blossoms and brothers in mixed beds etc.

as what concerns the sinking of tablets into the fold-depths of garments, so says the composer, they seem to be accompanied by the sounds of the Wesendonck-Lieder, the rustling of treetops in the garden, the bourgeons of chestnut-shoots as outstretched armlets in a vase

NAMELY THE POUT, that feeling-, taste-, smell-arousal from the ceaseless thumping of droplets out of the water line into the half-full sink in which the bouquet of anemones : still bound together, the stem wrapped with wet newspaper, this bouquet of torn blossom leaves, tenderly fringed, in the colors red rosy orange, because I was too tired, the bouquet into the flower vase : the floor vase to be filled with water then to *arrange* the bouquet while the *garment* of a flower condition a presentation of chocolate of pastry crumbs in a paper bag, wherein she, the pianist, struck the keys—so it was late in the night as the pianist bowed forward over on her low piano chair, nearly touching the floor with her knees in the enraptured pose of a Glenn Gould, his humming genuflection before the instrument etc., from kissing his neck, so says the pianist, from kissing the beloved on an admired area of the neck, which he let happen with closed eyes, namely open goblet or gullet of a white anemone, so says the pianist, and I to the *singspiel window*, so says the pianist, since I walked in the parlor where 1 flake lighted upon my curls but to me the rivers rustled, namely in their worldand

mit ihren Knien in der hingerissenen Haltung eines Glenn Gould, seinem summenden Kniefall vor dem Instrument usw., vom Küssen seines Nackens, so die Pianistin, vom Küssen des Geliebten an einer *bewunderten* Stelle seines Nackens, was er geschlossenen Auges geschehen liesz, nämlich offener Kelch oder Kehle einer weiszen Anemone, so die Pianistin, und ich ans *Singspiel Fenster*, so die Pianistin, da ich ging in der Stube wo mich 1 Flocke traf an meinen Locken aber es raschelten mir die Flüsse, nämlich in ihrer Welt- und Blumen-Verlorenheit. Ich öffnete die russ.Schokolade, und es fielen die Rippen, in schwarzes Silberpapier gehüllt, in meinen Schosz, so der Komponist, der Rhein schosz dahin und Clara nestelte das Neugeborene in ihrer Schlüsselbeingrube an ihrer rechten Brust dasz es nicht frieren sollte, es gab eine *differance* (Jacques Derrida) zwischen »o. T.« und »titellos«, dieses monströse »o. T.«, so der Komponist, erinnert freilich an l'art pour l'art, nämlich an den reglosen NUSZWALD wenn man den Hang der Nuszbergstrasze herniederwallt, usw., während Blumen und kl. Krebse, Äpfel und Weihwasserbecken auf dem Gemälde ein Stilleben darstellen, ich lag jedoch eines Morgens *im Schosz der Familie*, so der Komponist phantasierend, und wünschte mir einen Orgasmus – hier schieszen mehrere Erfahrungen zusammen, er hatte sich nachts entkleidet, den Überzug der Bettdecke heruntergerissen, dasz er wie 1 Bündel in der Ecke des Zimmers lag, in meiner Jugend war ich *sportiv*, so der Komponist, besonders liebte ich das Schwimmen das Springen (vom Turm vom Trampolin) das Innehalten im Sprung nämlich der Absprung der den Sprung in der Schwebe hält, man flog wie 1 Pfeil man taumelte in die Tiefe, bin Hysteriker man tauchte wieder auf, *der Text ist traubenförmig* (Jacques Derrida)

ich schleifte mein Holzbein nach, so der Komponist, ich war männlich geworden, ich hatte *eine Fliedertraube* zwischen den Beinen, was wehtat, war magnetisiert, da war doch dieser an der Frontseite des Briefes von Clara gedruckte Engel, der mit

flowerforlornness. I opened the Russian chocolate, and thus fell the strips, wrapped in black silver paper, into my lap, so says the composer, the Rhine dashed on and Clara nestled the newborn in her clavicle pit at her right breast that it shouldn't freeze, there was a *differance* (Jacques Derrida) between »untitled« and »title-less«, this gargantuan »untitled«, so says the composer, of course recalls l'art pour l'art, namely the motionless NUTWOOD when 1 streams down the slope of the Nuszbergstrasze, etc., while flowers and hl. crabs, apples and hl. water basin in the painting depict a still life, nonetheless I lie *in the lap of the family* 1 morning, the composer fantasizing so, and wished me an orgasm—here multiple experiences run together, he had unclothed himself at night, torn the cover from the bedding, that he lay in the corner of the room like a bundle, in my youth I was always *sportive*, so says the composer, I especially loved swimming diving (from the tower from the springboard) coming to a hold in the jump namely the jump-off that keeps the jump in suspense, 1 flew like an arrow 1 plummets into the deeps, am hysteric 1 resurfaced, *the text is grape-cluster-shaped* (Jacques Derrida)

I lugged my peg leg behind me, so says the composer, I had become masculine, I had *1 lilac grape* between the legs, which hurt, was magnetized, but still there on the frontside of the letter from Clara was this stamped angel, who with a quill pen from their pennage carves into the wax platter, namely writing thereon the music, as the young disc jockeys in the discotheques, etc., 4 months after Christmas the pine needles in my bed, so says the composer, when I look through my compositions, they seem UNFAMILIAR to me, strolled a lot today, Morandi painted only bottles, dream of banknotes between the sheet music, *I am your ivy now*, Robert so to Clara, the Icelandic ash cloud has reached Europe—as the angel of the gramophone concerns the angel of the disc, so says the composer, he either writes with a

einem Federkiel aus seinem Flügelkleid die Platte ritzt, nämlich die Musik darauf schreibt, wie die jungen discjockeys in den Discotheken, etc., 4 Monate nach Weihnachten die Tannennadeln in meinem Bett, so der Komponist, wenn ich meine Kompositionen durchsehe, kommen sie mir UNVERTRAUT vor, heute viel spaziert, Morandi hat nur Flaschen gemalt, träume von Geldscheinen zwischen den Notenblättern, *ich bin jetzt dein Epheu*, so Robert zu Clara, die isländische Aschewolke hat Europa erreicht – was den Engel des Grammophons den Engel des Discus angeht, so der Komponist, schreibt er mit einer Feder aus seinem Federkleid oder Flügelkleid auf die Schallplatte, er schneidet mit seinem Federkiel die Rillen in die Schallplatte, er kratzt die Musik aus der Schallplatte, wie 1 discjockey, aber es blutet das Morgenrot, so der Komponist, es läuten die Sterbeglöckchen des Windes, so bin ich in Tränen

was die Flüchtigkeit des Gemüts angeht, so der Komponist, musz das Werk den Erzeuger überschreiten oder überbieten, dann erwache ich beim geträumten Anblick eines weiszen Biedermeier Körbchens gefüllt mit duftenden rosa Magnolienblüten, beim UMGANG am Fronleichnamsstag, usw.

was die Schere auf dem offenen Soffa angeht, so der Komponist, *beherzigte* ich dasz ich ins Messer falle. Jenes Gefühl einer *Erweckung* durch das pausenlose fallen der Wassertröpfchen aus der Wasserleitung nämlich ins halbvolle Becken in welchem der Strausz Anemonen, noch zusammengebunden mit Hanf, die Stengel mit nassen Zeisigen umwickelt, dieser Strausz zerrissener Blütenblätter, allzumüde, die Blumen in die Bodenvase, nämlich die Blumen zu arrangieren während das Gewand eines Zustandes

ach er weinte sich die Augen aus, so die Pianistin, die Augen rutschten aus den Höhlen und auf die Wangen herab, also es tropften die Augen aus seinen Augenhöhlen und rutschten auf die Wangen herab, so die Pianistin –

pen from his pennage or wing-dress on the record, he cuts the grooves into the record with his stylus, he scratches the music out of the record, like a deejay, but it bleeds the break of day, so says the composer, thus ring the tiny death bells of the wind, so I am in tears

as what concerns the fleetness of mind, so says the composer, the work must transcend or surpass the maker, then I awake looking at the dreamed sight of a tiny white Biedermeier basket filled with fragrant rosy magnolia blossoms, while the PROCESSION on Corpus Christi Day, etc.

as what concerns the scissors on the open sofa, so says the composer, I *took to heart* that I was falling upon the knife. That feeling of an *awaking* through the ceaseless falling of water droplets from the water line namely into the half-full sink in which the anemone bouquet, still bound together with hemp the stems wound in wet siskin, this bouquet of torn blossom leaves, all too tired, the flowers in the floor vase, namely to arrange the flowers while the garment of a condition

ach he cried his eyes out, so says the pianist, the eyes slid out of their sockets and down onto the cheeks, i.e. the eyes dripped from their sockets and slid down onto the cheeks, so says the pianist —

as what concerns the mulberry treeling in the corner of the concert hall, the loving proceeding with it, the watering the touching the stroking of its leaves etc., are preconditions for its flourishing, so says the pianist, a ways across, straight across, over the Linzer Hauptplatz onward was atremble, 1 *christmas tree alley* palpable 1 turnaround before the hotel 1 rabbit (screaking) of the streetcar over the rails, I mean the Linzer Hauptplatz was such a charming grounds, so says the pianist, that every evening concert there, every meeting with Stifter

was das Lorbeerbäumchen in der Ecke des Konzertsaales angeht,
ist der liebevolle Umgang mit ihm, das Gieszen das Berühren das
Streicheln der Blätter etc., Voraussetzung für sein Gedeihen, so
die Pianistin, weit über, quer über, den Linzer Hauptplatz hinweg
sei 1 Zittern, 1 *Christbaumallee* spürbar gewesen 1 Kehrt-
machen vor dem Hotel 1 Kaninchen (Knirschen) der Straszen-
bahn in den Geleisen, ich meine der Linzer Hauptplatz sei 1
so hinreiszendes Areal gewesen, so die Pianistin, dasz jeder
Konzertabend dort, jedes Zusammentreffen mit Stifter und
seinem Schoszhündchen dort, 1 heimliches Fest, vor welchem
1 Damasttischtuch usw., *1 Kaninchen der Straszenkreuzun-
gen* dort, so die Pianistin, den Anfang eines Traumes ankün-
digte nämlich das Ausbreiten eines weiszen Damasttischtuch-
es, solcherart dasz die Pianistin vor jedem Konzertabend das
weisze Damasttischtuch in die Luft warf dasz es wölbte und
wölkte dasz es faltenlos NIEDERKOMME so dasz es beinahe
in der Luft des Saales stehenblieb und zwar eine längere Zeit
in der Luft stehenund hängenblieb und sich über der langen
Tafel niederliesz also sich ausbreitete NIEDERKAM wie 1 Wol-
ke : 1 Gewitterwolke der Töne, während ich den Verlauf des
Abends an Robert schrieb und welche seiner und Johannes
Brahms' Kompositionen den meisten Beifall, etc., während
das Knirschen der Trambahn eine Störung während des Kon-
zertes, so die Pianistin, verursachte wobei der Lorbeerkranz auf
die Stirn der Pianistin gedrückt ich meine was das Ergötzen des
lauschenden Publikums angeht. Während die hellbraun gesp-
renkelten zierlichen Pantöffelchen der abgefallenen Blütenblätter der Magnoliensträusze nach dem Konzert, so die Pianistin – was das tiefe Eindringen was das *Untertauchen* der
Tabletten in den Gewändern des Komponisten angeht, so
wurde es begleitet vom Schütteln des Kopfes des Komponisten seinem Summen und *Lamentieren* – drauszen die DEMO
in vollem Schwung, drinnen op.25/1, »du meine Seele« Stim-
mung und Veilchen Verhalten, er habe Musik *gedacht*, so Franz

and his tiny lapdog there, 1 secret celebration, before which 1 damask tablecloth etc., *1 rabbit of intersections* there, so says the pianist, the beginning of a dream namely the outspreading of a white damask tablecloth, such that before each evening concert the pianist threw the white damask tablecloth into the air that it vaulted and somersaulted that it should DESCEND foldless so that it all but came to a stand still in the air of the hall and indeed stood still and hung fast for a longer time and settled down over the long tabletop i.e. spread itself out DESCENDED as 1 cloud : 1 stormcloud of sound, while the course of the evening I wrote to Robert and which compositions of his and Johannes Brahms's the most plaudits, etc., while the screaking of the tram a disruption while the concert, so says the pianist, caused wherein the mulberry wreath pressed onto the pianist's forehead I mean as what concerns the rapture of the wide-eared audience. While the lightbrown sprinkled slipperlets of fallen blossomleaves from the magnolia-sprays after the concert, so says the pianist—as what concerns the deep permeation the tablet's *submergence* into the garments of the composer, it was thus accompanied by the composer's shakes of the head his humming and *lamenting*—the DEMO in full swing outside, op.25/1 inside, »du meine Seele« mood and violet demeanor, he *thought* music, so said Franz Liszt. A few hours later cooled spalliard : noted (nestled) down with distresses and flood of tears, however without emotion jotted typed—it was now with sign language that he : when something dissatisfied him he *shooed* it away with a hand motion, e.g. when all too shrill the sun fell onto his bedstead and the like.

I'm so involved with flowers, with weeping flowers, so says the pianist, after I had injured my hand 2 × on purpose, so says the composer, I hit on a book on which 1 bleeding hand was depicted, bandaging was made for him too of violet-bouquet and birdeye-speedwell, so says the pianist, binding/bandaging

Liszt. Ein paar Stunden später erkaltetes Spalier : mit Erschütterungen und Tränenstrom aufnotiert (genestelt), jedoch ohne Emotion reingeschrieben /getippt – er hatte es jetzt mit der Gebärdensprache : wenn ihm etwas miszfiel *verscheuchte* er es mit einer Handbewegung, z. B. wenn die Sonne allzu schrill auf seine Bettstatt fiel und dgl.

Ich habe so viel mit Blumen zu tun, mit weinenden Blumen, so die Pianistin, nachdem ich mir die Hand 2 × mit Absicht verletzt hatte, so der Komponist, stiesz ich auf ein Buch auf welchem 1 blutende Hand abgebildet war, man machte ihm auch Wickel aus Veilchenstrausz und Donnerblümchen, so die Pianistin, man machte mir auch Windel / Wickel und BINDEN in meiner damaligen Pubertät, vielleicht etwas Heiliges aber auch Anstösziges, das ich verbergen wollte, ich schämte mich zutiefst für diese blutgetränkten Bandagen, durfte sie auch nicht wegwerfen sondern muszte sie in einen Bottich mit kaltem Wasser TUNKEN und waschen, 1 grausame Aktion, sodann auf dem Dachboden wo Stricke gespannt waren, aufhängen. Diese Architektur von Gegenständen in meiner Behausung, so die Pianistin, diese ihre fragile Statik, so dasz man nicht daran rühren durfte, *Stiefmütterchens Gedanken* ich habe mich totgeschlafen, so der Komponist, linker Arm eingeschlafen Kopf ihn lange gepreszt

dann bin ich in das Pferdegespann hineingelaufen, so der Komponist, der Schatten der Amaryllis auf dem Fliesenboden des ORKUS

März/April 2010

and PADS were made for me too during my puberty at that time, perhaps something holy but something disagreeable too, which I wanted to hide, I was utmost ashamed of these soaked blood-bands, was not permitted to throw them away either but had to DUNK them in cold water and wash them, 1 dreadful act, so then to the attic where tightly drawn cords were strung, there to hang. This architecture of objects in my abode, so says the pianist, this her fragile static, so that 1 was not allowed to touch it, *heartsease thoughts* I slept myself to death, so says the composer, left arm fallen asleep head having long compressed it a long time

there I ran into the team of horses, so says the composer, the shadow of the amaryllis on the tile floor of the UNDERWORLD

March/April 2010

VOM UMARMEN DES KOMPONISTEN AUF DEM OFFENEN SOFFA

das Lorbeerbäumchen spricht zu mir sehr leise man hört es kaum es drück
sich grün in die Ecke des Zimmers oh sage ich wie schön du bist sein
Blattwerk reglos 1 wenig wie Säge wie Schleier wie Sprache wie grüner
Schnee ich halte ihm grüne Lettern vor seinen Leib dasz es erzittert
ich streiche ihm über seine Mähne dasz es erzittert es schaut es schaut
mich an obwohl hatte heute auf Klavier innig gespielt usw., 1 wenig
wie Brennesselfigur seine Figur seine Finger wie Brunnengrün tief wie
das grüne Wasser von alten Brunnen (neben der Kate), weiszt du noch sage
ich zu ihm damals in den Holundernächten den Liliennächten als der
Mond in eine Wiege damals als es ächzte im Gezweig der beiden Birnbäume
vor dem Tor. Ich schenkte ihm auszer einem Dante und Ariost seiner ....
und seiner Schwester Photographie mit entblösztem Haupte (wie wir
es vorgehabt hatten nicht wahr)
alles aus Einsamkeit komponiert heute ½ 5 Uhr morgens

19. 2. 2010

FROM EMBRACING THE COMPOSER ON THE OPEN SOFA

the mulberry treeling speaks to me so softly 1 hardly hears it pushes
itself green into the corner of the room oh I say how beautiful you are its
leafwork motionless a little like sawblade like veil like language like green
snow I hold green letters out to him before his body that it trembles
I stroke along the mane of his hair that it quivers it looks it looks
at me although had played inly on piano today etc., a little like
stinging-nettle-figure his figure his fingers like wellspring-green deep like
the green water of old wellsprings (by the cottage), do you remember I say
to him that time in the elderberry-nights the lily-nights as the
moon in a cradle that time it creaked in the branches of the two pear trees
at the gate. Along with a Dante and Ariosto I gave him his .....
and his sister's photograph with the bared head (as we
had intended to isn't it true)
all of it composed from loneliness 4:30 this morning

19. 2. 2010

ABOUT THE AUTHOR

Born in Vienna, Austria in 1924, FRIEDERIKE MAYRÖCKER has written over 100 works of poetry and prose among children's books, librettos, and radio plays. She is the recipient of countless prizes and awards, including the most important prize for German language literature, the Georg Büchner Prize. Mayröcker's collections available in English translation include *Night Train* (1992, trans. Beth Bjorklund); Heiligenanstalt (1994, trans. Rosmarie Waldrop); *with each clouded peak* (1998, trans. Rosmarie Waldrop and Harriett Watts); *peck me up, my wing* (2000, trans. Mary Burns); *Raving Language: Selected Poems* 1946-2006 (2007, trans. Richard Dove); and *brütt, or The Sighing Gardens* (2008, trans. Roslyn Theobald); *A Requiem for Ernst Jandl* (2018, Roslyn Theobald); and *Scardanelli* (2018, Jonathan Larson).

ABOUT THE TRANSLATOR

JONATHAN LARSON is a poet and translator living and working in Brooklyn. His translations of Francis Ponge's *Nioque of the Early-Spring* and Friederike Mayröcker's *Scardanelli* were published by The Song Cave.

ABOUT THE PRESS

OOMPH! is an international literary press publishing contemporary poetry and short prose in translation. Editors Daniel Beauregard and Alex Gregor founded the press in Argentina in 2014 with one aim in mind—to find new literature written in countries around the world and facilitate its translation into English. The editorial team currently operates across three continents to realize this goal as part of a larger mission to encourage cross-cultural and -linguistic exchange. Find out more at www.oomphpress.com.

Printed in Great Britain
by Amazon

87670290R00031